QUICK GUIDE
TO FEDERAL JOBS

QUICK GUIDE
TO FEDERAL JOBS

What you need to know to obtain a Federal job

BIANCA J. GORDON

iUniverse, Inc.
Bloomington

Quick Guide to Federal Jobs
What you need to know to obtain a Federal job

iUniverse books may be ordered through booksellers or by contacting:

iUniverse
1663 Liberty Drive
Bloomington, IN 47403
www.iuniverse.com
1-800-Authors (1-800-288-4677)

ISBN: 978-1-4759-2907-2 (sc)
ISBN: 978-1-4759-2908-9 (ebk)

Printed in the United States of America

iUniverse rev. date: 05/23/2012

INTRODUCTION

This guide is intended to teach my readers about the Federal application process. Although the process is quite complicated to someone without experience in applying for these positions, after reading this guide it should be much easier.

Although this guide covers the majority of positions within the Federal government, it is not intended to be all-inclusive. Each agency has its own hiring process and may differ from the process discussed.

The most important thing to remember is to read each announcement in its entirety and follow instructions, which are included. Most agencies will not make exceptions for applicants that fail to follow all of the instructions in the how to apply section of the vacancy.

Numerous applicants that were completely confused about the Federal hiring process planted the seed for this book. I saw the need for an explanation of the process without requiring the reader to dedicate hours of their time to read and still not get a good understanding.

Encouraged by my husband of ten years, Alan Gordon, I took up the venture to write this guide. Without his unwavering encouragement and support, I would not have taken this process up on my own.

I would like to thank three of my co-workers who also encouraged me in having this book published. Thank you to Amy Leonard, Denica Collins-Black, and Sharon Rodriquez. May this book assist you as well.

ABOUT THE AUTHOR

Bianca Gordon has spent sixteen years in various Human Resources functions. Upon entry into the United States Army, she began her career as a Human Resources Specialist. Her final three years in the Army were spent as a Recruiter where she decided to continue her career in the staffing arena.

Since leaving the Army in 2005, she has been in various functions of Human Resources and her last two years have been spent in Staffing for the Federal Government.

She is currently considered a journeyman in her career field and is dedicated to assisting others in obtaining Federal positions.

CONTENTS

USEFUL LINKS

---

www.usajobs.gov—Lists current Federal job openings and gives ability to apply.

www.opm.gov—links to useful information, benefits, laws, etc.

http://www.opm.gov/oca/12tables/index.asp—salary tables.

http://www.opm.gov/staffingportal/vetguide.asp—useful information for military veterans

http://www.usajobs.gov/StudentJobs—information for students and recent graduates.

BASICS

OVERVIEW

While there are several different types of appointments within the Federal government, this guide discusses only white-collar positions covered by Title 5 within the General Schedule pay scale. Title 5 covers the majority of positions within the Government and covers positions such as Secretaries, Program Support Specialists, Management Analysts, Human Resources Specialists, etc. The guide will cover only basic information needed to understand and apply for Federal positions. If you would like more information please visit **www.opm.gov. w**ww.USAJOBS.gov is the **primary** web site for Federal job announcements located in the United States and around the world. While it does not contain every job announcement from each agency, it is an excellent place to begin. Job announcements can also be found on the agency-specific websites. It is a good idea to search each individual agency web site for positions that may not be listed on www.USAJOBS.gov.

Applying for a position within the Federal government can be an overwhelming and frustrating experience, especially if you are unaware of the ins and outs of the application process. Many people are unaware of all the steps required and exactly how the process works. Within the next few chapters, I hope to enlighten my readers and hopefully aid some with obtaining a Federal position.

RESUME

The most important document of your application for Federal employment is your resume. The majority of applicants do not understand the difference between a Federal resume and a private sector resume. There are several distinct differences.

A private sector resume should be short and to the point. Recruiters and Headhunters will tell you that your resume should be no longer than one or two pages, and cover your past experience in less than thirty seconds. If it does not pass the thirty second test, your resume may very likely end up in the garbage.

When writing your Federal resume, you will need to be far more specific and detailed. The best way to write your resume is to think about every detail of your job and jotting it down on a piece of paper. Once you have written down the details, review them for accuracy and ensure you have covered all of your duties. One of the biggest mistakes most candidates make when applying for a position is not listing all of their experience.

The need for a longer resume is justified by the fact that Human Resources Specialists (Staffers) are governed by Federal laws and regulations as well as Union agreements; therefore they are not able to use their own subjectivity. If specific experience is not mentioned in an applicant's resume, then staffers have to determine that they are not qualified for the position.

With each position you have held, you will want to go into extreme detail regarding your experience. There is an example that I give to potential employees when discussing how detailed a resume should be, which I will give you as well.

If you are a Diagnostic Radiologic Technologist and you have worked in an Orthopedic Clinic, you may have had to clip someone's toenails in order to get proper positioning for the X-Ray. You will actually want to mention that specific detail within your resume. Another example is if you were previously employed as a secretary; do not just write a phrase that you performed administrative duties associated with your position. You will want to go into specifics, such as: assisted with the production of newsletters, and website revisions; maintained outlook calendars and scheduled appointments; prepared photocopies, facsimiles, scanning and filing; etc.

When listing your previous employment, ensure that you list the starting month and year of employment as well as your ending year. You will also want to put your salary and the hours per week worked for each position. This will allow staffers to calculate your years of experience. If for some reason you leave out the dates, you will find yourself found ineligible a lot of times due to the fact that it is indeterminable how much experience you actually possess. Your past salaries are also important; they are sometimes used to determine which level your prior positions were at. Salary is not the only determinant in deciding whether you are qualified for a position, but is certainly taken into consideration.

The average Federal resume is between five and ten pages depending on your past experience. There is no requirement for the length of your resume, but the more specific and detailed you are about your experience, the more you will find yourself qualified for jobs to which you apply.

When you look at a vacancy announcement, pay special attention to the major duties and specialized experience section. If you have indeed performed those duties you will want to ensure that they are reflected in your resume.

Do not use acronyms within your resume. They may make sense to you and within your industry, but are not familiar to those outside of the industry. You may use acronyms in parenthesis after you spell them out. This is especially true if you have been in a highly specialized field or in the military. Everything within your resume should be easy to read.

In order to give you an idea of what the differences are between a private sector and Federal positions, sample resumes are included on the next few pages. First, a sample private sector resume, then a Federal resume. Notice that the Federal resume is much lengthier than the private sector resume. The average Federal resume is usually between five and ten pages long, depending on experience. It is not unusual to receive resumes that are much longer than that. There is no specific criteria for how your resume should be formatted, but the more information you include, the better your chances at getting past the staffer and being certified to the selecting official.

Ms. Flowery Garden, PHR

1756 Petunia Street ♦ Las Vegas, NV ♦

(800) 555-5555 ♦ ILoveFlowers@hotmail.com

HUMAN RESOURCES SPECIALIST

- **Certified Professional in Human Resources (PHR)** offering an 18-year HR career distinguished by commended performance and proven results.

- **Extensive background in various HR duties**, including experience in employee recruitment and retention, staff development, benefits and compensation, HR records management, HR policies development and legal compliance.

- **Demonstrated success in negotiating win-win compromises**, developing teambuilding programs, and writing personnel manuals, corporate policies, job descriptions and management reports.

HR Skills

HR Department Startup	*Staff Recruitment & Retention*	*Training & Development*
Employment Law	*Benefits Administration*	*Performance Management*
FMLA/ADA/EEO/WC	*HR Program/Project Management*	*Organizational Development*
HR Policies & Procedures		

PROFESSIONAL EXPERIENCE

FLOWER PARADISE—Las Vegas, NV
<u>HR Specialist</u>, September 2010 to Present

Recruited to help open new hospital in Las Vegas, guiding the startup and management of a full spectrum of HR operations, systems and programs. Worked with senior management to create HR policies and procedures; recruit employees; and determine best recruitment method for hard-to-fill positions.

Key Experience:

- Key personnel in the recruitment/staffing of new hospital, which required the hiring of 700 new medical facility personnel within a one-year time frame.

- Performed internal/external placement duties, including carrying out special placement activities and provided interpretation and assistance on agency Merit Promotion program.

- Coordinated and executed plans to initiate and maintain a highly visible recruitment program to stimulate interest and attract qualified applicants for a variety of hard-to-fill occupations.

- Utilized a high degree of skill and professionalism in making personal contacts and dealing with representatives of medical/health organizations, hospitals, educational institutions, professional or trade associations, public employment services and other activities necessary to develop viable recruitment sources and to attract potentially qualified applicants.

- Reviewed and used job analysis processes to identify, analyze, and assess knowledge, skills, and abilities needed to perform a variety of positions.

- Provided managers and employees with information and interpretations of the organization's HR policies, procedures, and guidelines, when the issues addressed required substantial interpretation.

- Performed thorough analysis of operating procedures and mission requirements to accurately identify problems and to develop feasible and long-term solutions.

- Utilized a high degree of skill and professionalism in making personal contacts and dealing with representatives of medical/health organizations, hospitals, educational institutions, professional or trade associations, public employment services and other activities necessary to develop viable recruitment sources and to attract potentially qualified applicants.

FLOWER HEAVEN—Various Locations

HR Spec. (Recruitment), 02-05 HR Generalist, 91-95	Supv. HR Specialist, 95-02

Provided a broad range of HR functions, including recruiting and training employees, administering benefits, overseeing disciplinary action and managing HR records. Received numerous citations for exemplary service and outstanding performance.

Key Experience:

- Supervised the activities performed in all work units within an office, including office management, implementation of procedures, case management and processing, records management, collection and reporting of statistics, and accounting functions.
- Directed and evaluated the work of professional and technical human resources staff members, provided technical expertise to staff, and established section and staff work programs and objectives.
- Trained new staff members in human resources techniques and methodologies, oriented staff with appropriate laws, policies, regulations, and procedures, and ensured that work conformed to standards, regulations, and laws.
- Served on committees and built and maintained effective relationships with managers and other stakeholders in order to discuss and resolve issues/concerns, exchange information, and recommend changes to improve human resource programs and services.
- Networked through industry contacts, association memberships, trade groups and community leaders.
- Coordinated and implemented college recruiting initiatives.
- Conduct regular follow-up with managers to determine the effectiveness of recruiting plans and implementation.
- Developed a pool of qualified candidates in advance of need.

EDUCATION & CERTIFICATIONS

HORTICULTURE UNIVERSITY—FLOWER, USA

Bachelor of Science (BS) in Human Resources Management, Dec 2011

HR Designations:

PHR (Professional in Human Resources), 2011

Flower Rose Garden, PHR

1756 Petunia Street

Las Vegas, NV

(702) 555-5555

ILoveFlowers@hotmail.com

Objective

To obtain a position in Human Resources which works toward creating and supporting an environment that attracts and retains high performance professionals as well as developing processes and systems that align individual contributions toward the achievement of the organization's strategic goals.

Professional Experience

Flower Paradise   **07/31/11-Present**

Human Resources Specialist (Recruitment)

GS-0201-11/1—40 Hours per week

- Key personnel in the recruitment/staffing of new hospital, which required the hiring of 700 new medical facility personnel within a one-year time frame.
- Performed internal/external placement duties, including carrying out special placement activities and provided interpretation and assistance on agency Merit Promotion program.
- Determined the degree of compliance with regulations and other related requirements for programs assigned.
- Reviewed draft regulations, standards for impact on service organizations.
- Coordinated and executed plans to initiate and maintain a highly visible recruitment program to stimulate interest and attract qualified applicants for a variety of hard-to-fill occupations.
- Utilized a high degree of skill and professionalism in making personal contacts and dealing with representatives of medical/health organizations, hospitals, educational institutions, professional or trade associations, public employment services and other activities necessary to develop viable recruitment sources and to attract potentially qualified applicants.

- Regularly incorporated new recruiting authorities and laws into recruitment and placement efforts and made suggestions regarding recruitment incentives to attract applicants.

- Developed and published vacancy announcements and other recruitment materials using the latest technology.

- Reviewed and used job analysis processes to identify, analyze, and assess knowledge, skills, and abilities needed to perform a variety of positions.

- Rated and examined applications against minimum qualification standards, including selective factors.

- Used and developed criteria for evaluating the extent to which applicants possess job related knowledge, skills, and abilities, and ranked eligibles accordingly.

- Reviewed the results of the selection process for compliance with regulatory selection rules, laws, and regulations.

- Made appropriate salary determinations for each appointment in accordance with governing regulations.

- Developed all staff work including recommending the best method of filling vacancies.

- Independently researched and resolved all but the most unusual placement problems.

- Anticipated the need for outside and/or special recruitment efforts, in particular, consideration of responsibilities under Affirmative Action, FEORP, and Handicapped placement plan and developed appropriate outside recruitment sources.

- Provided advisory service and assistance to management and employees for a variety of personnel programs.

- Provided managers and employees with information and interpretations of the organization's HR policies, procedures, and guidelines, when the issues addressed required substantial interpretation.

- Established and maintained a cooperative working relationship with managers.

- Performed thorough analysis of operating procedures and mission requirements to accurately identify problems and to develop feasible and long-term solutions.

Flower Haven   **11/07/10-07/30/11**

Human Resources Assistant (Recruitment)
GS-0203-06/1—40 hours per week

- Performed work associated with Merit Promotion and placement actions involving internal applicants.

- Worked with managers to develop recruitment strategy, discussing all available options to ensure maximum regulatory and procedural flexibility is utilized in meeting the manager's needs.
- Developed and posted vacancy announcements ensuring compliance with labor contract and applicable regulatory requirements.
- Responded to applicants' questions regarding the application and qualification process.
- Evaluated applications for eligibility, time-in-grade, time-after-competitive appointment, basic qualifications, and other pertinent legal and regulatory requirements and refer eligible candidates to selecting official, ensuring that best-qualified determinations or paneling occur as required.
- Made job offer to selected candidates and negotiate release date with gaining and losing managers.
- Completed SF-52, "Request for Personnel Actions" for selected candidate(s).
- Provided guidance to coding staff in the entry of the action.
- Confirmed selections and notify non-selected candidates in writing.
- Closed out files, ensuring file retention met regulatory requirements.
- Responded to requests for routine technical advisory services on Merit Promotion, recruitment, position classification, and position management issues received via phone or e-mail from managers, HR and payroll employees at VA field facilities, and other customers.
- Performed appropriate regulatory research to ensure accurate, timely advice is provided to requester.
- Provided interpretation of agency policies and procedures to managers and employees.
- Ensured all actions are properly documented to meet legal and regulatory requirements.
- Worked with managers to ensure timely, accurate processing of SF-52s for other internal placements and pay administration actions.
- Ensured proper documentation is obtained for voluntary actions requested by employees.
- Coordinated delegated examining unit requests, when applicable.

Bianca J. Gordon

Daisyland   **09/27/10-11/06/10**

Office Automation Assistant GS-0326-05/1—40 hours per week

- Used the full range of functions, including advanced processes, of one or more desktop publishing applications to produce a variety of documents.

- Typed, edited, formatted and printed a wide variety of documents for the office staff, including correspondence, reports, technical notes, presentation and briefing material in accordance with established guidelines and procedures. Source materials are either written drafts or voice recordings.

- Operated a computer, peripheral equipment and appropriate software to perform various computer operations in support of office operations, such as producing reports, maintaining databases, and travel order information.

- Maintained and updated computer user manuals, reference books and operating handbooks.

- Used basic and advanced program functions to perform such operations as updating and researching for and retrieving data for reports.

- Reviewed forms, documentation, and other related information from inmates, victims, witnesses and other civilian and military agencies and constructed various types of records or files.

- Researched and/or provided factual information regarding directly applicable rules, regulations, procedures, and requirements to provide explanations of actions taken or recommended

Rose Enterprise   **08/07-09/10**

Human Resources Assistant GS-0203-05/5—40 hours per week

- Provided information, guidance, and administrative assistance to all Army Service Members.

- Received and input information regarding soldiers' personnel records into database in order to produce DD Form 214.

- Informed personnel of benefits, which they were eligible for upon discharge from the Army.

- Maintained internal database to ensure proper tracking/accountability of personnel files.

- Monitored/reviewed the Military Personnel Records Jacket of all Active Duty and National Guard soldiers receiving discharge from the military.

- Counseled soldiers on pay entitlements based on family structure, family location, grade, and years of service.
- Assisted with implementing and maintaining family support services.
- Coordinated with community agencies assists the Rear Detachment Commander (RDC) in the preparation, coordination of briefings, orientations, and workshops, informing soldiers and family member regarding the functions of the Family Readiness Program and a variety of deployment and reunion issues.
- Maintained day-to-day awareness regarding public, military, and/or administrative issues impacting the families of deployed military personnel.
- Assisted the RDC in instructing/training units, soldiers, and their families on Family Readiness issues.
- Maintained regular telephonic/electronic contact with the unity Family Programs Assistant to receive technical support of family readiness activities and issues.
- Performed word-processing functions, type forms, and maintains files.
- Prepared and distributed written information such as flyers, letters, calendars, and newsletters.

Lilly World   **05/05-05/07**

Human Resources Specialist (Recruitment/)—40 hours per week

- Provided support in functional areas of HR (Operations, Administration, or Sales) including, but not limited to employment, personnel records, employee and labor relations, health and welfare benefits administration, organization development, training, and special projects.

- Managed contact with prospective employees and assured interested candidates were informed of appropriate policies and application procedures.

- Coordinated and executed plans to initiate and maintain a highly visible recruitment program to stimulate interest and attract qualified applicants for a variety of hard-to-fill occupations.

- Determined the degree of compliance with federal hiring regulations.

- Utilized a high degree of skill and professionalism in making personal contacts and dealing with representatives of architectural and engineering organizations, educational institutions, and professional organizations.

- Incorporated new recruiting authorities and laws into recruitment efforts.

- Provided managers and employees with information and interpretations of the agency's recruitment policies, procedures and guidelines.

- Maintained current knowledge of recruitment trends and best practices through review of current research/studies and professional literature.

- Reviewed recruitment actions and provided continuing technical advice and assistance in resolution of recruitment problems for a wide variety of engineering occupations.

- Evaluated the correctness and propriety of actions taken in terms of conformance to available guides.

- Provided staffing and placement advice, assistance and support under the general supervision of a senior specialist.

- Assisted in the development and implementation of HR policies and procedures and their dissemination through employee booklets, communications, and/or meetings.

- Educated new hires on all aspects of benefit programs encouraging employees to fully utilize and appreciate available benefits.

- Resolved employee relations matters through coaching and counseling. Work with managers and employees to formulate fair solutions that preserve all party's dignity and respect.

- Recruited, interviewed, and evaluated candidates to determine qualifications for employment under current staffing laws and regulations.
- Wrote and placed advertisements in print media, company web site and online job boards.
- Communicated and administered various HR plans and procedures for company personnel.
- Updated job descriptions and performed job analysis as necessary.
- Acted as HR liaison for management of functional areas (Operations, Sales, or Administration).

Carnation Passion   **9/99-5/05**

Recruiter—40 hours per week

- Evaluated human relations and work related problems and met with supervisors and managers to determine effective remediation techniques.
- Developed and conducted training to instruct establishment managers, supervisors, and workers in human relation skills such as supervisory skills, conflict resolution skills, interpersonal communication skills, and effective group interaction skills.
- Reviewed employment applications and evaluated work history, education and training, job skills, compensation needs, and other qualifications of applicants.
- Performed reference and background checks on Interviewed military and civilian personnel to recruit and inform individuals on matters concerning career opportunities, incentives, military rights and benefits, and advantages of military career applicants.
- Informed applicants of job duties and responsibilities, compensation and benefits, work schedules and working conditions, company and union policies, promotional opportunities, and other related information.
- Searched for, interviewed, screened, and recruited job applicants to fill existing company job openings.
- Recorded additional knowledge, skills, abilities, interests, test results, and other data pertinent to selection and referral of applicants.
- Occasionally lectured to civic and social groups, military dependents, school officials, and religious leaders concerning military career opportunities.
- Arranged for skills, intelligence, or psychological testing of applicants.

Tulip Treasury   **02/97-9/99**

Supervisory Human Resources Specialist—40 hours per week

- Supervised the activities performed in all work units within an office, including office management, implementation of procedures, case management and processing, records management, collection and reporting of statistics, and accounting functions.
- Served as first-line supervisor and technical expert in the various areas of human resources;
- Planned, organized and directed the activities of the branch, ensuring that work complied with legal and regulatory requirements and meet the needs of customers.
- Provided advice and consultative services to employees and managers to carry out the functions of the branch.
- Established, developed and maintained effective working relationships with customers at all levels.
- Met with key customers to assess customer satisfaction, explained organizational policy and procedures and resolved problems that arose.
- Rendered authoritative advice and guidance to staff, employees and management officials to support the goals and the objectives of the organization.
- Established metrics and analyzed systems to ensure actions, advice and services were timely and were reviewed at critical points.
- Determined appropriate corrective actions or areas of focus for continued improvement;
- In a supervisory capacity, planned and assigned work to subordinates.
- Assured that subordinates were adequately trained to perform assigned duties and recommended additional training when needed.
- Evaluated performance and resolved conduct or performance related issues.
- Guided staff in the formulation of management's position regarding persistent laws, rules, regulations, and Executive Orders affecting overall program effectiveness.
- Established guidelines and performance expectations for staff that are clearly communicated through formal and informal performance management evaluations.
- Reviewed and/or drafted standard operating procedures and other written documents based on subject matter expertise, knowledge of existing internal procedures and awareness of current regulatory or legal requirements.
- Provided manager with technical interpretations of policies and procedures when the issues involved were new, highly controversial, precedent setting and/or involved implications in more than one subject matter area.

- Stayed abreast of changes in federal and agency human resources regulations and policies to ensure that processes and procedures were adjusted as needed to comply with those changes.

- Performed administrative and human resource management functions relative to staff supervised, establishes guidelines and performance expectations for staff that are clearly communicated through formal and informal performance management evaluations.

- Exercised the full range of supervisory human resources management responsibilities.

- Assisted in the overall management of all military human resources programs.

- Skilled in working with persons at various levels and backgrounds.

- Directed and evaluated the work of professional and technical human resources staff members, provided technical expertise to staff, and established section and staff work programs and objectives.

- Planned, assigned, and reviewed the work of staff members performing a variety of human resources functions and recommended changes in practices and procedures to increase operating efficiency and expedite work flow.

- Trained new staff members in human resources techniques and methodologies, oriented staff with appropriate laws, policies, regulations, and procedures, and ensured that work conformed to standards, regulations, and laws.

- Reviewed new policy proposals or revisions and made recommendations about their effectiveness.

- Served on committees and built and maintained effective relationships with managers and other stakeholders in order to discuss and resolve issues/concerns, exchange information, and recommend changes to improve human resource programs and services.

- Ensured that staff prepared comprehensive records, reports, and documentation that complied with standards and requirements.

- Developed or modified work plans, methods, and procedures and determined work priorities.

- Assigned and distributed work, reviewed work for accuracy and completeness, and returned assignments with recommendations for proper completion.

- Resolved problems encountered during daily operations and determined standards for problem resolution including escalations.

- Developed the performance enhancement plan, documented performance, provided performance feedback, and formally evaluated the work of employees.

- Documented causes for disciplinary action and initiated letters of reprimand and formal recommendations for disciplinary action.

- Provided work instruction and assisted employees with difficult and/or unusual assignments.

- Performed personnel administrative tasks, including coordinating and participating in the hiring and promotion process, supervising the training of new employees and the ongoing training of other employees, resolving unusual employee problems, and supervising employee time and attendance records.

- Trained staff in the use of automated systems and word processing software introduced new versions or functions, trouble shot problems, and attended meetings.

- Interpreted and explained personnel rules and transaction procedures to department heads, employees, and applicants.

- Demonstrated continuous effort to improve operations, decrease turnaround times, streamlined work processes, and worked cooperatively and jointly to provide quality seamless customer service.

Perennial Paradise   **06/91-02/97**

Human Resources Specialist—40 hours per week

- Processed, controlled, verified, and issued identification cards for active duty, reserve, and national guard members, military retirees, and family members/dependents, Government civilian employees, and contracted employees.

- Issued memorandums of authorization for Commissary and Post Exchange to eligible customers.

- Registered, processed and maintained the Defense Enrollment Eligibility Reporting System (DEERS) and the Real-Time Automated Identification System (RAPIDS) as part of a Verifying Official's responsibilities.

- Performed routine operator maintenance on RAPIDS workstations and printers, i.e. changed lamination, added toner, cleaned printers, etc.

- Responsible for the control and issue of identification tags and Geneva Convention cards when authorized to military members, deploying civilian employees, and other eligible recipients.

- Performed all ID Card and CAC issuance related tasks to include researching and reviewing source documents, verifying eligibility, and discussing entitlements.

- Prepared, updated, and coordinated requests for evaluations, to include responding to evaluation inquiries.

- Prepared and monitored requests for promotions and arranged for promotion ceremony, to include promotion declinations, reconsideration for promotions, and arranged for reduction and removal boards for soldiers on local promotion standing lists.
- Prepared and monitored requests for reductions, transfer, and discharges.
- Prepared and monitored requests for identification cards and tags, leaves, and passes, line of duty determination, MILPER data and information management, orders for temporary duty and travel, personnel processing, personnel Security Clearances, training and reassignment, retention, military and special pay programs, personnel accounting and strength management, transition processing, legal, meal cards, training soldier support file, and unit administration.
- Evaluated personnel qualifications for special assignment.
- Prepared orders and request for orders.
- Prepared and maintained officer and enlisted personnel records.
- Processed recommendations for awards and decorations, processed bars to reenlistment, suspension of favorable personnel actions.

Education & Training

B.S.B.A—Human Resources Management, Horticulture University 01/2012.

Additional Information

Professional in Human Resources Certification—05/2011
Nationally recognized as Top Producing Recruiter in March of fiscal year 2003.
Consistently recognized as Top Producing Recruiter at Regional level for fiscal year 2003.
Recognized as Top Producing Recruiter at Company level every month throughout fiscal year 2003.

PAY PLANS

There are many different pay plans within the government such as General Schedule (GS), the Federal Wage System (FWS), or the Senior Executive Service (SES), covers most positions within the Federal government.

The General Schedule (GS) consists of 15 grades, each broadly defined in law in terms of work difficulty, responsibility, and the qualifications required for performance.

The Federal Wage System (FWS) pay plan covers trade, craft, and labor occupations in the Federal Government. There are three pay scales within the FWS. The non-supervisory, non-lead employee is considered a Wage Grade employee and the pay designation is WG. The wage grade consists of 15 grades, each broadly defined in law in terms of work difficulty, responsibility, and the qualifications required for performance. The second pay scale within the FWS covers Leader positions and the pay designation is WL and has the same 15 grades as the WG pay plan. Supervisory positions have a pay designation of WS and it has 19 grades.

The Senior Executive Service (SES) covers most managerial, supervisory, and policy positions, which are classified above the GS-15 pay grade and do not require Senate confirmation.

The Office of Personnel Management's (OPM's) Web site hosts the salary and wage tables for most major pay plans, which is located at www.opm.gov.

EDUCATION

Although education is a wonderful thing, the Federal government prefers experience over education in most positions. There will be positions that have a positive educational requirement, but it is usually expected that you have at least a couple of years of experience.

For the most part, a bachelor's degree will qualify you for a GS-5 and a master's degree for a GS-7. There are times when a bachelor's degree will qualify you for a GS-7 and a master's degree will qualify you for a GS-9, but that is only when the degree actually relates to the position. For example, a bachelor's degree in Business will qualify you for a GS-7 in Human Resources, but a bachelor's degree in Sports Medicine will not.

If you plan on using your education to qualify, make sure you upload or fax your unofficial transcripts according to the vacancy announcement instructions. If you do not include your resume, education will not be used to determine qualification.

SPECIALIZED EXPERIENCE

Specialized experience will be determined by the information within your resume. There are varied amounts of experience required for each grade. For example if a position is a GS-5, usually you are required to have approximately one to one-and-a-half years of experience relating to the position. For this example, let's assume that the position is a multi-graded career ladder position. This means the position has promotion potential to GS-9. The position may be announced as a GS-5/7/9 or GS-5 Target 9. To be eligible for the GS-7 position, you will need to have at least two years of experience and for the GS-9 you will need at least three years of experience.

You may also find positions which are graded GS-5/6/7 or GS-5 Target 7, where again the requirement is one year for the GS-5 level, two years for the GS-6, and three years for the GS-7.

You will find all of the information within the vacancy announcement. In the next chapter, I will explain how to read an announcement to assist you in locating the area of the vacancy where you would find that information.

TIME-IN-GRADE REQUIREMENT

The Time-In-Grade requirement only concerns current Federal employees or persons who have held a Federal position within the last 52-weeks. The requirements state that you must have at least 52-weeks (one-year) time in your current grade before you are eligible for promotion to the next grade. There are two ways to circumvent the time-in-grade requirement, if you are a VRA eligible candidate, or if the vacancy is announced through DEU, which will be discussed in a later chapter.

The Time-In-Grade requirement goes into effect on the first day of employment, so if you receive another offer for a higher graded position prior to your first day, you will not be required to complete 52-weeks at the lower grade. Once you begin your first day of work, you are subject to the rule and are only able to circumvent it through a DEU announcement or if you are VRA eligible.

ANNOUNCEMENT

READING AN ANNOUNCEMENT

In order to apply for a position, you must first know how to read the announcement. Within the announcement, you will find all of the information you need, to determine eligibility for the job that you are applying to. Below you will find each section of the announcement with a brief explanation of what it means.

Job Title: The job title will be the first component of the announcement. The information provided here will give you the official job title and sometimes the occupational series and grade.

Department: This is the department of an agency, or sub-agency.

Agency: The agency is the Federal organization.

Job Announcement Number: The job announcement number is a number assigned to the position, which aids the agency in tracking the status of the announcement. This number is very important if you call or e-mail the agency regarding the status of your application. Without the job announcement number or the vacancy ID number, you may have trouble keeping your application information organized.

Salary Range: Even though this seems self-explanatory, there are several factors involved in determining your salary. If you have not worked for the Federal government before, under Title 5 laws, you will almost always come in at the lowest salary, unless other specific guidelines are met. If you are being reassigned, promoted, or transferred, within the Government, then your salary is dependent on your current salary as well as Federal Pay Setting rules.

Open Period: These are the dates applications will be accepted for the position. Applications and/or resumes will not be accepted after the closing date, unless you are at least a 30% disabled Veteran with documentation.

Series & Grade: The occupational code and grade are listed here. For example GS-0201-13; GS is the pay scale, which stands for General Schedule. 0201 is the Human Resources Specialist career field, and 13 is the pay grade.

Position Information: The terms of the position are listed here, they may state Full-Time, Part-Time, Permanent, Temporary, etc.

Duty Locations: Where the position is located. Most of the time the location is very specific, but you will find positions that have various or several locations. Pay close attention to this part, because you do not want to apply for a position in Timbuktu, if you are not willing or able to relocate.

Who May Be Considered: This is an extremely important area to pay attention to. If this section reads, "Status Candidates," it means that only personnel who are already working for the Federal government and certain special hiring authority eligibles (such as VRA, VEOA, Schedule A, etc.) will be considered for this position. There is no possibility for the position to open up to outside candidates due to way Federal regulations are written when it comes to position announcements. If you apply for a position for which you are not eligible to apply for, you will receive a rating of IVCA (some agencies may use a different code,), which stands for, "Ineligible, Outside of the Area of Consideration." I will get into detail regarding special hiring authorities in the next chapter. If for some reason there are not enough candidates or the selecting official wants a larger choice, then he/she may go DEU (which means it is open to the public and has its own announcement number.)

Key Requirements: Key requirements inform the applicant of items required for the positions, i.e. Pre-employment physicals, drug testing, background investigations, and/or citizenship requirements.

Duties: You will find some of the duties that you will be required to perform if you are selected for the position. Be advised that not **ALL** duties will be listed here; it is just a sampling of what will be essential to accomplish your daily mission.

Qualifications Required: These are the minimum requirements you will need to meet in order to be eligible for the position. This section will vary from position to position, as well as from agency to agency. Usually educational requirements, experience requirements, and/ or certification or licensing requirements will be discussed in this section as well. Many times you will find examples of specialized experience within this section as well. The specialized experience is the previous experience required for you to be qualified for the position. Your resume must indicate that you have had experience performing these duties, or you will not be considered qualified for the position.

How You Will Be Evaluated: This is an explanation of how your qualifications are determined and possibly give you some additional instructions.

Benefits: Some of the benefits offered by the agency will list here.

How To Apply: This may be one of the single-most important areas of the announcement. Many applicants fail to follow instructions and lose consideration due to that fact. Here you will find instructions on where and how to apply for the position. Most agencies prefer the online application method. Pay special attention to the required documents section; many agencies will not consider you for the position if you do not submit all required documents. If you are not sure that you have supplied all of the necessary documents, contact the agency and ask them to take a look at your application to determine whether all document requirements have been fulfilled.

Agency Contact Info: Contact information will be listed here. Agencies will list information such as contact name, contact telephone, e-mail address, etc. This will be the person you would call or e-mail with questions concerning the vacancy.

APPLYING FOR THE POSITION

When you are ready to apply for a specific position and have located it on www.USAJobs.gov, you will open the announcement and click on the "Apply Online" button. At this juncture you will be required to log in to the website with your Username and Password.

The first section will give you the option to select one of your stored resumes. Click on your preferred resume to highlight the option. You will then follow the same procedure for the attachment(s) section. Underneath both tables, you will find three written sentences with selection boxes to the left of them. After reading each statement, check the boxes and click on "Apply for this position now!"

You will now be brought to the system used by the agency to complete your application process. Most agencies use Application Manager, but some still have their own preferred systems. Here we will assume that the agency you are applying to uses Application Manager. Click on the "Proceed with my Application" tab.

The first page you will encounter will ask you for biographic data. Here you will enter your address, telephone number, contact time preference, fax number, e-mail address, work information, and citizenship information. After responding to all areas, click "next."

Now you will be asked questions regarding your eligibility. Ensure you read each question carefully, as skipping questions or not checking the appropriate boxes can determine whether you are going to be found qualified for any special hiring authorities. Click "Next."

This section will ask you about your availability date and Job Related Experience. You may leave these sections blank if you do not wish to answer. Click "Next."

The next section is the Assessment Questionnaire also called Occupational Questionnaire. These sections may contain as few as two or three questions up to one hundred or more. Read each section carefully, as each response is used in grading your application and determining eligibility. Do not blindly click on responses without reading the question in its entirety. Continue through each section until you come to the "Reuse Documents" section.

If you have previously used Application Manager to apply for positions, you will have documents available for re-use. If you have included all of the documents you wish to add when you made your resume selection, you will not need to add them again. Click "Next."

Here you will have the opportunity to upload additional documents you wish to use. This section is very helpful if you have never used the document before and did not have the document saved to your "Saved Documents." Add any documents you wish to add and click "Next."

Now that you have answered all of the occupational questions and added all of your documents you will come to the "Submit My Answers" screen. Click on "Submit My Answers." Your application is **<u>NOT</u>** complete until you do so. You have now completed the application process. If you would like to view or print your answers you will be able to do so at this time.

AFTER YOU APPLY

Once you have completed the application process, the waiting begins. Most agencies prefer that you track and monitor application manager to ensure you've submitted all of your documents, if you are uncertain about whether you have submitted all of your documents, contact the Human Resources Department listed on the announcement to ask if all of your documents have been submitted. Ensure you have the Vacancy ID or Announcement number handy, since the person will most definitely ask you for it when looking up the position.

Once the position application period closes, the HR Department will determine qualifications on each applicant. This can take a few days up to several months depending on various factors such as workload, priorities, number of applicants, position approval, etc. Once the qualifications have been determined, you will receive correspondence from the agency regarding qualifications. If you are sent forward to the selecting/hiring official, they will contact you if an interview is required. After all interviews are completed, it may take an additional time period before job offers are made depending on agency policy, etc. If you are selected, you will more than likely be notified telephonically. If you are not selected, you will usually receive e-mail.

If you have questions regarding your qualifications and/or selection status, contact the HR Department

SPECIAL HIRING AUTHORITIES

WHAT ARE SPECIAL HIRING AUTHORITIES?

Special Hiring Authorities are used by agencies to appoint specific groups of individuals who meet the respective eligibility requirements to positions in the Federal Government. Using these authorities can give you the opportunity to apply for positions to which you would normally not be eligible for. The most common authorities are as follows:

Schedule A: This special hiring authority can be used to hire applicants with mental retardation, severe physical, or severe psychiatric disability to fill a job which the person is able to perform. If applying under Schedule A, a letter from a physician must be accompanied with the application stating the applicant is eligible for non-competitive appointment using Schedule A.

Schedule B: Generally this hiring authority is used for students to fill positions. Only students qualify for these programs and must submit documentation to prove status.

Veterans Employment Opportunities Act (VEOA): This special hiring authority is available to veterans who are either "preference eligible," or who have substantially completed three or more years of active service. VEOA allows veterans to apply for positions that are only open to status candidates. You must provide documentation to prove eligibility.

Veterans' Recruitment Appointment (VRA): VRA is an excepted authority, which allows eligible veterans to be appointed to a position without competition. VRA also allows the veteran to circumvent time-in-grade requirements for positions up to GS-11. To be eligible for VRA the following provisions apply: be in receipt of a campaign badge for service during a war or in a campaign or expedition; or are a disabled veteran; or are in receipt of an Armed Forces Service Medal for participation in a military operation; or are a recently separated veteran (within the last 3 years); and separated under honorable conditions.

30% Disabled Veteran: 30% or more Disabled Veteran allows any veteran with a 30% or more service-connected disability to be non-competitively appointed. You are eligible if you retired from active military service with a service-connected disability rating of 30% or; or you have a rating by the Department of Veterans Affairs showing a service-connected disability of 30% or more. Using this authority, an agency can make permanent, temporary, or term appointments in the competitive service. There is no grade level restriction.

Delegated Examining Unit

DEU

Positions are announced either through the Delegated Examining Unit or Merit Promotion. There are very distinct differences between the two, which confuses the majority of people.

Delegated Examining Unit (DEU)

The Delegated Examining Unit (DEU) is a way for the Government to recruit outside of its current workforce. Anyone who is a United States citizen may apply, and in some cases nationals and non-citizens may apply as well—although those cases are rare. The rules and regulations that cover DEU are somewhat confusing, but some of the main ones will be covered to clear up some of the perplexity.

Veterans Preference

Veterans' preference applies when hiring is completed through the DEU. This by no means signifies that veterans are entitled to a position, nor that they are qualified simply based on the fact that they are veterans. A preference veteran must still qualify for the position as set forward by the qualification standards for the occupation.

To receive preference, a veteran must have been discharged from active duty in the Armed Forces under honorable conditions. Military retirees at the rank of major, lieutenant commander, or higher are not eligible for preference in appointment unless they are disabled veterans. The types of preference available for veterans are:

5-Point Preference (TP)—Five points are added to the **PASSING** score or rating of a veteran who served during a war; or during specific periods of time; or in a campaign or expedition for which a campaign medal has been authorized. There is additional criteria, which can be found at www.opm.gov/staffingportal/vetguide.asp

10-Point Compensable Disability Preference (CP)—Ten points are added to the **PASSING** score or rating of a veteran who served at any time and who has a compensable service-connected disability rating of at least 10 percent but less than 30 percent.

10-Point 30 Percent Compensable Disability Preference (CPS)—Ten points are added to the passing score or rating of a veteran who served at any time and who has a compensable service-connected disability rating of 30 percent or more.

10-Point Disability Preference (XP)—Ten points are added to the **PASSING** score or rating of a veteran who has a service-connected disability rating of less than 10 percent or has received a Purple Heart.

10-Point Derived Preference (XP)—Ten points are added to the **PASSING** examination score or rating of spouses, widows, widowers, or mothers of veterans as described below, however, neither may receive preference if the veteran is living and is qualified for Federal Employment.

Spouse—Ten points are added to the **PASSING** score or rating of the spouse of a disabled veteran who is disqualified for a Federal position along the general lines of his or her normal job because of a service-connected disability. If the veteran is working, the spouse is not entitled to this preference.

Widow/Widower—Ten points are added to the **PASSING** score of the widow or widower of a veteran, who was not divorced from the veteran, has not remarried, or the remarriage was annulled. Other stipulations apply. Please visit www.opm.gov/staffingportal/vetguide.asp for additional requirements for this preference.

Mother of a deceased veteran—Ten points are added to the **PASSING** score or rating of the mother of a veteran who died under honorable conditions while on active duty during a war, or in a campaign or expedition for which a campaign medal has been authorized. Other criteria apply. Please visit www.opm.gov/staffingportal/vetguide.asp for additional requirements.

Mother of a disabled veteran—Ten points are added to the **PASSING** score or rating of a mother of a living disabled veteran if the veteran was separated with an honorable or general discharge from active duty. Additional criteria apply. Please visit www.opm.gov/staffingportal/vetguide.asp for additional requirements.

When applying for a position and you wish to use veteran's preference, you must include all documentation proving you are eligible for the preference. If proper documentation is not included, your application will be viewed as a non-preference candidate. For required documents, please either review the announcement, or call the Human Resources office that is responsible for the vacancy. The Human Resources office will not contact you if you fail to submit all documents. As the applicant, it is your responsibility to ensure your application is complete.

MERIT PROMOTIONS

MERIT PROMOTIONS

Merit Promotions are covered by different rules and regulations than DEU positions. Merit Promotions cover positions that are open to current Federal employees and /or VEOA, VRA, 30% disabled veterans, Military Spouses, and Schedule A applicants.

Although certain veterans may apply for these positions, veteran's preference does not apply. This means that everyone will be considered equally based on qualifications and performance.

If applying for Merit Promotion positions, you MUST meet time-in-grade as well as specialized experience to be eligible. The only exceptions are VRA which can be promoted to GS-11 without meeting the time-in-grade requirement, and 30% disabled veterans which do not need to meet this requirement regardless of which grade they are applying to. Please remember, all candidates must still meet specialized experience no matter what. There are no exceptions to this rule! As always, if you have any questions regarding your eligibility, contact the Human Resources office that handles the position that you are interested in.

MILITARY VETERANS

TIPS FOR VETERANS

As a military Vetcran, I found it extremely hard to adjust to the civilian way of thinking. Many of us spend a good time of our lives in uniform and have no idea of how to adjust to civilian life. I have included some helpful tips for you to navigate the federal job market.

Rank/Grade: After serving in the military, you should be proud of the rank or grade you have achieved. You worked hard for it, bled for it, and sweated for it. Now you are looking for civilian employment and are unsure of how your position in the military will convert. First thing I would like to mention is that there is no GS equivalent to military pay grades, even though many want to believe it and spread this rumor. The DOD will sometimes make a GS grade comparison when the assignment is overseas and they wish to put you in acceptable level living quarters. These are not circumstances that arise on a typical basis. Some agencies look for certain pay grades in the military for specific positions, but most your experience will be in your resume.

Resume: Do yourself a huge favor and do not clump your entire twenty-year career into one paragraph. There is no way you can articulate all of your experience in a few sentences. Separate each one of your assignments into its own section. Even if you were an Infantryman, you may not have fired the same weapon at each duty assignment. Even if your military occupational specialty is one that does not convert, usually there have been instances when you worked in an office environment or were detailed to another position. This is very important to mention in your resume.

As I mentioned previously, you can never mention enough experience, even minute details can sometimes be used to qualify you for a specific job. If you are unsure of how you should articulate your experience you may want to visit your local VA that offers these services to military veterans, or visit the state offices that also provide these services. Good luck to you, and HOAAAAH!

FINAL THOUGHTS

There are several things you will want to keep in mind when applying for Federal positions. The main thing you will need is patience. Government jobs do not work like private sector positions and it may take several months in some cases to find out whether you were selected. If you ever have questions concerning a specific announcement, it is always a good idea to contact the Human Resources Office that is announcing the vacancy. Always remain professional and courteous to get the best results. Be tenacious with your applications, there is a lot of competition for almost every position available, but the more you apply and interview, the better you will get. Good luck to you all!

Printed in the United States
By Bookmasters